MASTERING BITCOIN COMPLETE GUIDE TO MINING CRYPTOCURRENCY AT A PROFITABLE TIME

EASILY CREATE YOUR OWN MINING RIG

By

MITCHELL WILSON

CentrallyDecentralized.com

INTRODUCTION

"Mining is the art of exploiting mineral deposits at a profit. An unprofitable mine is fit only for the sepulcher of a dead mule."
— T.A. Rickard

Reading this book I assume you aspire to become a cryptocurrency miner or to possibly get a better idea about what this mad bitcoin frenzy is about? If you were to invest 100$ into Bitcoins in 2011 they would be worth millions today. I can guarantee you will hold a great understanding of the subject shortly and be on your way to making money. Cryptocurrency is not as hard to understand as others think and bitcoin is really just as hard as you make it. Before you know it you'll be setting up your own mining rig and making coins of your choice. The thrill and excitement of watching your bank account grow while you do nothing is irresistible, passive income made by mining coins may become a full time gig if you gain a passion for it like I have and learn some tips and tricks to getting the most out of your money that I'm excited to share with you.

Unfortunately bitcoin has gained an odd reputation to some people due to a lack of understanding. Cryptocurrency is seen as shady due to the misconceptions it's received, is this a BUBBLE? A Ponzi Scheme? Don't people use this to make anonymous illegal transactions? How can this just appear out of nowhere shooting from (at the time I bought my largest bitcoin amount) $5,000 to $20,000!? Well to put your mind at rest you must first understand the economics behind cryptocurrency and understand that its goal is to simply allow value to be transferred from one place to another without a 3-rd party drawing a percentage from the transaction.

Bitcoin hit record highs and was recognized as a system different than the world has ever seen before. Who would have thought such great technology was readily available years ago and just now is being recognized as a quick, cheap, international currency that puts other forms of currencies to shame.

TABLE OF CONTENTS

CHAPTER 1. WHAT IS BITCOIN?

Bitcoin has completely changed the way we think of money/currency and has started to shake the world making it's way into an immature market. Satoshi Nakamoto (the founder of Bitcoin) probably didn't expect this magnitude of growth in the what started as free of cost software project he developed in 2009. Something interesting to keep in mind is that bitcoin uses cryptography in order to verify its transactions. Cryptography is a method of storing and transmitting data in a particular form so that only those for whom it is intended can read and process it and this was actually used in World War II to send secret information from one party to another! Now for those being suspicious on the past bitcoin transactions used within the dark web, cryptography is coded to be readable by another party and the owner, and as time goes on we are able to trace current and past bitcoin transactions which have led to many criminals' incarceration. The process of verifying these transactions is where we get this simple process called bitcoin mining. This simple process sends the value from one address to another in a series of numbers and letters. *Ghi76fkdsbli7hliuhd78*. It looks like gibberish huh? Well this is the cryptography I was speaking of, and a bitcoin address. These transactions are stored on a gigantic ledger called the Blockchain which holds every transaction ever made with Bitcoin on public record! This system is made up of mining machines which run a type of software that both relay information and accept and verify a transaction.

This is where us miners get
our glory, bitcoin mining is simply just
verifying transactions made on the
blockchain network/ledger using computer
like machines and software. The miners
handle this great process by connecting to
something called peer-to-peer networks. To
understand a peer to peer network simply
think of two or more computers connecting
and sharing files/ resources without going
through a separate server. Sharing data has
never been easier, Bitcoin offers a supreme
service that will continue to operate on
Nodes across the globe until otherwise

proven useless. Yes, bitcoin is actually useful, but what the heck is a NODE!? Well to be put simply, a node is nothing but a system/computer that is involved in the Peer to Peer network. The way I picture nodes doing their "job" is by picturing a family tree, in my family tree I have distant relatives called cousins who are attached to other families that ultimately create a relation to that other family. Think of a node as the same way, a computer(node) won't have a direct relation to all other nodes but a select few which also have connections to other nodes that share the entire blockchain and that allows a type of communication to be established.

    Us miners make the blockchain go round and round by solving extremely complicated math problems or algorithms that tend to get more and more difficult as the blockchain is created. The solving of this complicated algorithm benefits the network by verifying transactions and creating what we call HASH which is simply a function that converts one value to another. I picture a hash in the form of coal mining as getting your paycheck at the end of the week, but in the case of bitcoin mining it's how we get paid. Solving these complex algorithms following this slightly confusing blockchain take computers, or machines that can push power which add the cost of hardware and electric consumption. If someone decides to mine cryptocurrency they learn there is a cost of hardware and the electricity cost to run the machine, which definitely isn't free, therefore a miner is rewarded with a portion of the coin he/she is mining as a type of reward system for the work their machines have put in based off the hash they have achieved. Now that you've got an idea of how the process works we can begin talking about how to stake your claim in the mining business and discover how to create a worthy source of passive income.

CHAPTER 2. WHY SHOULD I MINE?

There will only ever be 21,000,000 BTC found and as time goes on, they become harder and harder to mine. What does that tell me? Something is this popular and limited in resource? I'm actually surprised the price of Bitcoin hasn't reached over $20,000....

Considering the technology and innovation taking place, including the lightning network which is hailed to be one of the most important implementations to solve the issue of scaling allowing cheap and quick transactions on the blockchain. Combined with the fact that the CBOE is pushing the SEC for bitcoin ETF by the end of the year, investing now, while sentiment is low, could turn out to be one of the greatest buying opportunities we will ever see! I'm writing this book to help others have the same success I experienced and will soon benefit from again. I'll include my email at the end of this guide, I'd love to speak with you and help in any way I can. Most importantly I want to hear your success story of bitcoin, this changed my life and I know it will change yours. I've asked several of my friends in this industry why they chose to start verifying bitcoin transactions through mining and I've received different answers from "I'm all about the decentralization" while others believe in it as a solid investment, for myself, I just want to get my fix on this nerdy sweet tooth. On few occasions I've run into people who are well into the mining business stumbled upon it accidently be it something they were already doing merged as an extension to bitcoin, or a type of computer project such as grid due to it's fun of working in a community environment to solve the big picture. Bitcoins can be sent from anywhere in the world to anywhere else in the world. No bank can block payments or close your account. Bitcoin is censorship resistant money.

CHAPTER 3. HOW TO CREATE YOUR RIG

This is my favorite part of the book, the moment I've been waiting to get started on, creating you OWN mining rig. It's really not as difficult as they make it seem, it's practically just a gaming computer with a few different twists. The software can be pre bought or even programmed yourself if that's your thing. Building your rig is actually really simple if you follow this guide, now that you have a slight understanding of how the blockchain works it will be easier to understand the process of piecing the hardware together and knowing what each part does in this mining process. On top of that you'll be making your very own coin of choice right away! I started with an Antminer s9 from Bitmain, at the time I lived in a small apartment in a warm climate and the Antminer s9 pushed out much heat and was noisy so I decided to get rid of it and try and create my own machine, one that isn't loud and doesn't use as much electricity. Based on the watts the S9 consumed I wasn't making a big profit due to the electricity costs but it was something, I could see the true value in mining when bitcoin rose to $20,000 and I thought I landed on a gold mine, well bitcoin soon dropped and I was overjoyed I sold my Bitcoins when I did. The same time I started to mine bitcoin I became interested in the technology behind it and realized this was something amazing, and a new revolution was coming whether or not we are ready for it, decentralization. Proof to me that Bitcoin will soon become priceless was the combination of legendary technology and popularity, along with being the O.G. of cryptocurrency puts it with the comparison of gold. Let's get started on your rig, I'll lay it out piece by piece so it's easy to understand.

We will Start with the Motherboard and the GPU! The motherboard acts as almost a central control system connecting the parts together, when choosing
a motherboard you want to be sure it has the proper slots for the components that you'll be adding as well as being sure your model/brand of equipment works with the other. This isn't a very picky set of hardware which seems to be fairly interchangeable, especially with the use of adaptors. Mining rigs fall into different categories: CPU miners GPU miners and ASIC miners. A CPU miner uses the computer's central processor to do the mining and so a

powerful processor will give you more mining power while a gpu miner uses graphics cards for mining, so the central processor really only has to run the operating system and mining software and requires little processing power. The ASIC is more advanced and will be covered in my next guide as I'm currently building different types of mining machines experimenting with different parts.

Your motherboard will need to provide you with enough GPU slots to attach your Graphics Cards to. These graphic cards are typically used in videogames, but in our case this will be the algorithm problem solver. The better the GPU (graphics card) the better hash rate you will be able to achieve. you will want to find a motherboard with as many GPU slots as you plan on attaching. Choosing the graphics cards next requires some studying up to determine how much hash power you would like to push. Some graphics cards are expensive and may not put out much hash power while others at lower costs can prove to surprise you on what they can accomplish. I'll gladly list some of my favorites at the end of this book. Most graphics cards will have a different type of connector and won't be able to be plugged directly into the motherboard, well fear not! PCIE Risers are available for your purchase at a low cost, this will enable you to snap on and connect to the PCIE slot on the motherboard and allow you to attach multiple Graphics cards (GPU). It is extremely important that you use a powerful GPU or a set of GPUs to get the job done. I'll list some of my favorite parts and combinations at a different time. Understand that this hardware machine (miner) you are putting together will have electricity costs and it's your job as the miner to do the math (not difficult math like your machine's algorithms) but simple math, actually so simple you can type into your internet search bar "bitcoin mining calculator" it will automatically ask how much hash power you put out, and your electric usage in watts or kW so the hard work is done for you. You may find that it's better for you to use a series of gpus rather than one or two powerful ones. This part is pretty important, it's always good to figure out what your product will produce (if possible) before acting on it, it just simply saves you time and money. If you're like me you'll completely ignore that statement and dive in head first to get a feel for things, I don't blame those of you that follow that route you'll still be learning in a more exciting but less productive way. Keep in mind bitcoin mining gets more and more difficult everyday, the algorithms get harder and harder to solve as they get longer while being added to the blockchain making the process more difficult. The main things to consider with your GPUs is the Hash, this hash is equal to the amount of numbers your graphic cards can handle. The more hashes you have, or to put it differently, the higher your hash rate, the more efficient you will be. Hash is also labeled different ways you should be aware of, such as mHASH/j this type of hash is what your card/gpu is able to handle per unit of energy, while mHASH/s shows the performance that your card/gpu is putting out, the higher the number, the more money you'll be making, however watch out for high electricity usage that may offset your earnings. Currently some of my favorite Graphic Cards are the GeForce GTX 1080 TI, Radeon RX Vega 64, Radeon RX Vega 56, Radeon Rx 580, Radeon Rx 480,

Geforce GTX 1070, Radeon Rx 570, Radeon Rx 470, Geforce GTX 1060 and the Radeon R9 290x. These are current, and I know as this book ages new technologies and better cards will be created.

For motherboards I currently have successfully had luck with some of the following: Biostar TB250-BTC, Asus Prime Z270-P Motherboard, Asus Prime Z270-A Motherboard ,Intel Celeron G-3930, Intel Pentium G4400, Biostar TB-85 Motherboard , Asrock H81 Pro BTC Motherboard, and MSI Z170A TOMAHAWK Motherboard. If your motherboard doesn't include a processor, just simply pick up a Intel Celeron G1840 Processor or Intel Celeron G3260 Processor.

To power these components you'll need a Power Source Unit, or a PSU. Desktop computers usually stay between 250-500w but you're not running a desktop, your running a mining machine that powers gpus, and depending on the amount of gpus is the amount of power you will need. Plan anywhere between 800-1,000w for smaller miners, and 1200-1700w for larger mining systems. Power supplies have rating you should pay attention to, Gold, Platinum, and Titanium that will also factor into your electric usage cost. Power Source Units come in many different sizes so you can calculate what works best for you. For example, I found it profitable on one of my machines to run two 750w psu to the same mining machine. When choosing your PSU don't make the mistake like I did and only calculate the power consumption your graphics cards put out, this is wrong. It's a close measurement but you need to check ALL components of your mining rig and total up the total Watt usage before choosing a power source. In my case I had an underpowered rig which caused me a few annoying problems. Think about it this way, if you are using two different graphics cards that use 300W a piece, and you find that another part of the rig takes 300W well you're looking at a usage of 900W, so I would probably go with a 1,000W PSU. My choice list of PSU are some of the following: Silverstone Tek 1500W 80 PLUS Gold, Corsair AXi Series, 1500 Watt, 80+ Titanium Certified, Corsair HX1200 1200W 80+ Platinum, Seasonic Power supply Power Supply SSR-1200G, SilverStone Technology Strider 1200W 80 Plus Platinum, Silverstone Tek 1350W, EVGA SuperNOVA 1600 T2 80+ TITANIUM, EVGA SuperNOVA 1600 G2 80+ GOLD, Thermaltake 1200-Watt 80 Plus Gold, Thermaltake Toughpower DPS G RGB 1250W Digital 80+ Titanium, and the Thermaltake Tough Power Series ATX 12V 1200. This list could go on and on so experiment and search, just make sure it produces the power you need to meet consumption.

Next you'll need to go get yourself a hard drive, all this component does is stores your Operating System and your mining software that you choose to use. (mining software will be discussed further down) Decide how you want to mine, hardcore with many gpus or start out light? Either way you'll need a hard drive to prepare and operate your system. Depending on your mining preference you can probably get away with an 60 or 120 ssd drive or flash drive depending on how you'll be mining. I would recommend buying preloaded software that starts right up and begins mining immediately, or you can buy a drive and load your own software. While you're at it pick yourself up a simple stick of 4GB

DDR3 1600Mhz RAM, (Random Access Memory) you won't need more than this, and to help you understand it, it acts as a notepad, or dry erase board for your operating system, (even computers have to take notes). Lastly for hardware you'll want to purchase a Monitor, mouse, and keyboard, all of which can be cheap. These items are only used for setup and occasional updates, your machine will be doing all the complicated math problems!

The most rewarding part of the build for myself was the Case, the Case I built put everything into perspective and made it all seem real, I'll never forget the joy I felt from the first rig I built when I placed it on the case I built. You on the other hand don't have to build your own case, you can buy something at your local store that will hold your machine, such as a metal rack case, or something with shelves. When deciding on what type of case you'll have keep in mind the number of GPU's you are using and if you are using risers(adaptors) to plug in multiple GPUS. Having your GPUs apart from each other is important, on a mining rig you really don't want anything sitting on top of one another because they tend to get hot and that would be a fire hazard. I won't focus as much on the case as I'll let your creative juices flow so you may determine what's best for you. Now let's put these parts together and get you on your way to making some money!!

CHAPTER 4. PUTTING IT TOGETHER

You're almost there, well that is assuming you've collected all of the components listed above....Lets put it all together and start your mining. I also assume you've bought/ put your case together, make sure to keep your mining rig within decent ventilation so overheating doesn't occur. Place your hardware pieces on the case keeping the Graphics cards lifted above the motherboard or to the side. Your Graphics cards will most likely have fans to keep cool, so the more air the better. The PCIE Risers you should have bought will connect your GPU's to your motherboard without having to plug the GPU into the motherboard directly, that would cause a jumble. Your PSU will have connects with it that plug into the motherboard and GPUs, they are easy to figure out, easier than me writing it all out for you. If you can't figure it out within about 10 minutes I would refer to a youtube video, as most PSU hookups are done the same. Just type "putting my mining rig together" and you should have a quick concise video to visually show you. Once cords are attached you need to get the correct software for your machine. Don't worry, I won't go into too much depth. You can buy preloaded USB Flash Drives that will literally start mining the second you plug them in, so the software part has been configured for you already!

CHAPTER 5. SOFTWARE

As far as mining software and operating systems, I'll provide a few options starting with the most simple first. Preloaded mining software is available for your purchase on few different sites, the only one that comes to mind at the moment is Ethos, who offers preloaded USB flash drives that start up immediately when plugged into the usb port on your motherboard. Everything is taken care of for you, and you can get out for around $40. Check it out, I use the ethOS 16gb USB 3.0.

If you are more adept to technology, especially software I would run Linux/Ubuntu, however if you want something more simple just stick with the windows operating system because drivers update on their own. After some research on this topic I've actually found that if you're careful and look for it, there is free open software available for you to try. I see more and more pop up everyday so if you wanted to upload your own mining software you find to your flash or ssd, be my guest. Be careful to choose the correct mining software to go along with what you want to mine. Like I said, there are more and more types of software for different operating systems and/or different altcoins popping up everyday so if you're using windows and mining Ethereum make sure your software supports Etherium mining on windows. If you've chosen the software and preloaded onto your device it's now time to turn the mining rig on and check for updates/setup depending on the software and OS you've downloaded. If you aren't familiar with Ubuntu/Linux then you should just stick with windows as I said before, it just seems to run more smoothly for those of you who don't use Linux, there will be a time consuming learning curve there. Upon booting up your device you'll probably hear fans running on the PSU and GPU, this is normal, you did it! If they aren't spinning don't freak out, just look at your GPU/PSU settings and make sure they just come on when needed. It may be possible with your operating system you have updates, or must reflash the firmware (depending on your machine), it will be obvious as you'll see that on startup. Go through any needed prompts which should be few if any, your software provider may have a tool available for monitoring your miner's stats such as temperature and hash power. There are applications you can download on another device, such as a phone, which can track these stats for you. I'm just going to give Ethos as an example, buying their preloaded USB allows for an immediate startup. Their setup guide for their USB Flash Nano 3.0 consists of:

Quick Start Guide

1. Run helpme to get a list of commands, your stats panel link, and rig status.
2. **Force ethOS to keep local.conf changes after Reboots.**
3. In **/home/ethos/local.conf** , change "0x0bdC4F12fB57d3acA9C3cF72B7AA27 89A20d27f2" to your wallet (<u>Editing Files with Nano</u>).
4. Change **both** user "ethos" and superuser "root" password with passwd ethos and sudo passwd to secure your rig.
5. Reboot with r.

   NOTE: If you would like to reset all configs to their factory defaults, use reset-config.

   ethOS is set to mine to

the ethOS Ethereum pool. Check your mining statistics
at <u>http://ethosdistro.com/pool/</u>

I would recommend going with a preloaded drive, they take out all the difficult work for you. Most sites use a Username and Password which is the same to monitor your stats. You don't have to use eTHOS, like I said pick the type of software according to what you are using and mining for, their guide will be just as easy as the one you see above.

Once your mining rig is up and running you are now going to do a few small, quick things to get you started. First, you need to determine whether or not you want to mine in a pool or solo, most people will mine in a pool as it has proven to generate a better profit.

CHAPTER 6. SHOULD I MINE SOLO OR IN A POOL?

Solo mining is seen as both profitable and nonprofitable depending on how you look at it, you are trying to win a block within a certain amount of time, so the speed and power of your system is important when determining this, and a single system could take days, weeks, month, or years. The probability of mining a block solo is not high but the reward of winning a block is 25 BTC! Most people use pool mining, both large and small mining setups. Thanks to pooled mining we can team out systems together through a network and work together to win a block. This is cool because it increases the probability of winning a block due to all the systems hashing together, which creates a constant payout and eliminates risk. Mining pools are easy to join and readily available, they will provide you with an address to point your mining machine to, for example if you are mining bitcoin and want to use btcminer you will input this address into your miner.

us.ss.btc.com:1800

us.ss.btc.com:443

us.ss.btc.com:25

If you are unsure of how to do this figure out the IP address of your mining machine, it should be connected to your router via ethernet cable. Search online for your internet provider, or look on the side of your router for a username and password, type the URL you see on the router in your browser and enter your username and password that was seen on the side of your router.

You'll see the devices there, copy and paste the IP address of your machine. If the IP address asks for a username and password try admin as both username and password. If this is not the case, use an i.p. address finder tool and locate it quick and easily. If login to router doesn't work, call your internet service provider.

CHAPTER 7. CREATE YOUR DIGITAL WALLET

When I first discovered bitcoin and cryptocurrency there were only wallets available to store my coin online, now they have hardware wallets that provide incredible amounts of security compared to a digital wallet. Starting out, I would recommend opening a digital wallet with Coinbase. There are many types of digital wallets so read the terms and conditions before making your decision.

Type coinbase in your search engine on any device and download the app and sign up for an account. You'll be asked a series of questions just like anything you sign up for. You'll receive the key to your account which you should write down and keep somewhere safe. Your account will provide you with a send and receive address. You will want to visit the site/miner software you are using and input your receiving address key in the field where your software should say something like

Payment/Wallet/Account on the options/settings menu. You'll see an area to input your address to get paid your earnings into, and it works just like direct deposit. Congratulations, you are now making money while you sleep. Enjoy!

Email admin@centrallydecentralized.com for any questions or something I missed?
    Thanks For Reading, Good Luck on your mining journey!

Www.CentrallyDecentralized.Com

If you enjoyed this book, found it useful or otherwise then I'd really appreciate it if you would post a short review on Amazon. I do read all the reviews personally so that I can continually write what people are wanting.

Thanks for your support!

www.ingramcontent.com/pod-product-compliance
Lightning Source LLC
LaVergne TN
LVHW041221050326
832903LV00021B/734